MIGHTY MACHINES

Airplanes

by Mary Lindeen

BLASTOFF! READERS

BELLWETHER MEDIA · MINNEAPOLIS, MN

Note to Librarians, Teachers, and Parents:

Blastoff! Readers are carefully developed by literacy experts and combine standards-based content with developmentally appropriate text.

Level 1 provides the most support through repetition of high-frequency words, light text, predictable sentence patterns, and strong visual support.

Level 2 offers early readers a bit more challenge through varied simple sentences, increased text load, and less repetition of high-frequency words.

Level 3 advances early-fluent readers toward fluency through increased text and concept load, less reliance on visuals, longer sentences, and more literary language.

Whichever book is right for your reader, Blastoff! Readers are the perfect books to build confidence and encourage a love of reading that will last a lifetime!

This edition first published in 2007 by Bellwether Media.

No part of this publication may be reproduced in whole or in part without written permission of the publisher. For information regarding permission, write to Bellwether Media Inc., Attention: Permissions Department, Post Office Box 1C, Minnetonka, MN 55345-9998.

Library of Congress Cataloging-in-Publication Data

Lindeen, Mary.
  Airplanes / by Mary Lindeen.
    p. cm. — (Blastoff! readers) (Mighty machines)
Summary: "Simple text and supportive full-color photographs introduce young readers to airplanes. Intended for kindergarten through third grade"—Provided by publisher.
  Includes bibliographical references and index.
  ISBN-13: 978-1-60014-058-7 (hardcover : alk. paper)
  ISBN-10: 1-60014-058-0 (hardcover : alk. paper)
  1. Airplanes—Juvenile literature. I. Title.

TL547.L5935 2007
629.133'34—dc22   2006035260

Text copyright © 2007 by Bellwether Media.
SCHOLASTIC, CHILDREN'S PRESS, and associated logos are trademarks and/or registered trademarks of Scholastic Inc.
Printed in the United States of America.

Contents

What Is an Airplane?   4

Parts of an Airplane   6

A Trip on a Jumbo Jet   14

Glossary   22

To Learn More   23

Index   24

An airplane
is a machine
that flies
through the air.

An airplane has a **cockpit**. The **pilot** sits in the cockpit.

An airplane has wings. Wings help lift the airplane in the air.

wings

This small airplane has a **propeller**. A propeller helps this small airplane fly.

propeller

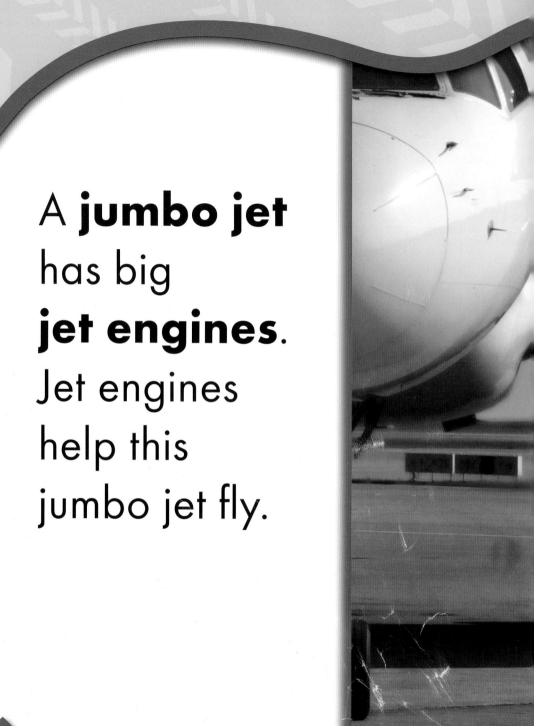

A **jumbo jet** has big **jet engines**. Jet engines help this jumbo jet fly.

jet engine

A jumbo jet holds many **passengers**.

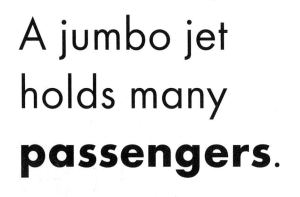

Passengers get on airplanes at an **airport**.

The airplane
gets ready
to take off.
It speeds down
the **runway**.

The wheels of
the airplane
lift off
the ground.
Take off!

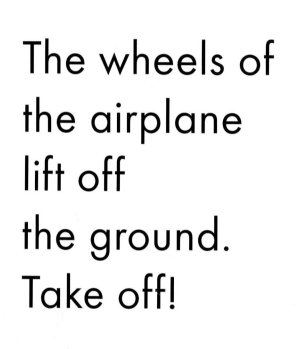

Glossary

airport—a place where airplanes take off and land and passengers wait for airplanes

cockpit—the front part of an airplane where the pilot sits

jet engines—machines that power a jet airplane

jumbo jet—a big airplane with a wide body

passenger—a person who rides in an airplane, car, truck, or boat

pilot—the person who flies an airplane

propeller—a pair of flat blades that turn in a circle and power an airplane

runway—a long, flat road where airplanes take off and land

To Learn More

AT THE LIBRARY

Liebman, Dan. *I Want To Be A Pilot*.
Willowdale, Ont.: Firefly, 1999.

Molzahn, Arlene Bourgeois. *Airplanes*.
Berkeley Heights, NJ: Enslow, 2003.

Williams, Zachary. *How Do Airplanes Fly*.
New York: Rosen, 2003.

ON THE WEB

Learning more about mighty
machines is as easy as 1, 2, 3.

1. Go to www.factsurfer.com

2. Enter "mighty machines" into search box.

3. Click the "Surf" button and you will see a
   list of related web sites.

With factsurfer.com, finding more information
is just a click away.

Index

air, 4, 8

airport, 16

cockpit, 6

ground, 20

jet engines, 12

jumbo jet, 12, 14

machine, 4

passengers, 14, 16

pilot, 6

propeller, 10

runway, 18

wheels, 20

wings, 8

The photographs in this book are reproduced through the courtesy of: Denise Kappa, front cover; vm, p. 5; Darryl Brooks, p. 7; Karen Hadley, p. 9; Roman Milert, p. 11; Mikael Damkler, p. 13; Johner/Getty Images, p. 15; APIX/Alamy, p. 17; Eric Gevaert, p. 19; Michael Rosa, p. 21.